Could it be? Had enemy spies sneaked into the United States? The country had not yet entered World War II, but had the war now come to American soil?

The Federal Bureau of Investigation (FBI) had intercepted hundreds of coded messages from a secret base in New York but couldn't read them. Someone had to crack the code. But who? The FBI turned to one special woman to decipher the secret messages . . .

EXA BKBJV PMFBP PKBXHBA QL QEB

FKQBOZBMQBA

FKQBOZBMQBA ERKAOBAP
INTERCEPTED HUNDREDS

LC ZLABA JBPPXDBP
OF

QL QEBAKFQBA PQ

EXA BJ

L ZOXZH QEB

The artwork in this book was painted by hand
in watercolor and gouache, and assembled digitally.

Cataloging-in-Publication Data has been applied for and may
be obtained from the Library of Congress.

ISBN 978-1-4197-3963-7

Text copyright © 2021 Laurie Wallmark
Illustrations copyright © 2021 Brooke Smart
Rhyming verse on final page by Leslie Tran
Book design by Heather Kelly

Printed and bound in China
10 9 8 7 6 5 4 3

Abrams Books for Young Readers are available at special discounts when purchased in quantity for
premiums and promotions as well as fundraising or educational use. Special editions can also be created to specification.
For details, contact specialsales@abramsbooks.com or the address below.

ABRAMS The Art of Books
195 Broadway, New York, NY 10007
abramsbooks.com

To my daughters, Kim and Lisa — L.W.

To my Mom — B.S.

XHBO, PMV ERKQBO : ELT BIFWBYBQE COFBAJXK ZE

CODE BREAKER, SPY HUNTER

HOW ELIZEBETH FRIEDMAN CHANGED THE COURSE OF TWO WORLD WARS

by Laurie Wallmark
illustrated by Brooke Smart

YV YOLL

FIIRPQOXQBA YV

HOXIIJXOH TXIIJXOH

JXROFB

YV JXROFB

Abrams Books for Young Readers • New York

"A cryptanalyst is a person who analyzes and reads secret communications without the knowledge of the system used."

Elizebeth Smith Friedman, a cryptanalyst with a stellar reputation, agreed to work with the FBI on their top-secret project. And once she'd broken the codes, she discovered the senders were indeed spies—Nazis! At the trial, the content of those deciphered messages provided the hard evidence needed to send thirty-three German spies to prison. According to the FBI, Elizebeth's work resulted in the "greatest spy roundup in American history."

And to think, if not for a chance encounter with a librarian more than twenty-five years earlier, Elizebeth might never have become a code breaker at all.

As a child Elizebeth loved to read, especially poetry.
One of her favorite poets was William Shakespeare.
His poetry showed structure and patterns, just like
she would later look for in coded messages.

"Why should something with a risk in it give me an exuberant feeling inside me?"

NIVERSITÄT

μαθησ

τοφία

CATIONEM

POESI

LINGUA

CHOLAE

ΚΟΛΛΕΓΙΟ

"My education as a whole was rather versatile in languages."

Fascinated with languages, Elizebeth majored in English
literature at college and also studied Latin, Greek, and
German. She graduated in 1915 and worked for a year
as a high school principal. After that, Elizebeth went to
Chicago, looking for a job in research or literature.

While in town, she couldn't wait to stop by the Newberry Library to see their famous collection of Shakespeare's plays. When Elizebeth mentioned she needed a job, the librarian introduced her to George Fabyan, an eccentric multimillionaire and fellow Shakespeare fan. Fabyan invited her to join other researchers at his Illinois estate, Riverbank. He was convinced Francis Bacon, a famous scientist and author, was the real creator of Shakespeare's plays. To prove this, Fabyan wanted Elizebeth to find secret messages Bacon had supposedly hidden in the plays.

Little did she know how peculiar her new boss would turn out to be.
Fabyan kept monkeys on his estate. He raised honeybees inside his house,
the Villa, because he didn't trust them to make honey unless he supervised.
Most unusual of all, he hung his furniture from the ceiling on chains.

The more Elizebeth studied the plays, the more she believed there weren't any secret messages.

She shared her suspicions with one of her scientist friends, William Friedman, and he agreed. Elizebeth and William's discussions soon changed from codes hidden in Shakespeare's plays to codes in general. They spent their free time indulging in their favorite game—writing secret notes and challenging each other to decode them. As their code making and code breaking skills grew, so did their friendship.

"So little was known in this country of codes and ciphers when the United States entered World War I, that we ourselves had to be the learners, the workers, and the teachers all at one and the same time."

Friendship turned to love, and within a year, Elizebeth and William married.

After the United States entered World War I in 1917, the government needed people to decode spy messages. Fabyan asked Elizebeth and William to set up the country's first code-breaking unit, the Riverbank Department of Ciphers. For eight months, the American military brought all secret enemy communications to Riverbank for decoding. Elizebeth, William, and their staff developed many new code-breaking techniques and authored eight pamphlets detailing them. Their methods are now considered the basis for the modern science of cryptology, the study of secret codes.

RIVERBANK

In 1921, Elizebeth and William moved to Washington, D.C., to work as code breakers for the Army communications department, the Signal Corps. Until then, the Army had used a simple machine, the teleprinter, to send messages. But, if the enemy intercepted the transmissions, anyone could read them, so the Army coded the messages first.

"our desk work ... at that time consisted in revising and creating new codes for army field use."

There was a problem, though. These machines were huge and could only be used in large office buildings. But soldiers needed to be able to send secrets from anywhere, even from deep within the jungles of far-off islands.

Elizebeth and William invented a scientific method to create complicated ciphers, a type of code, using only pencil and paper. Ciphers use secret rules for replacing each letter with a different one. If the enemy didn't know the rules, they would have a hard time figuring out the message.

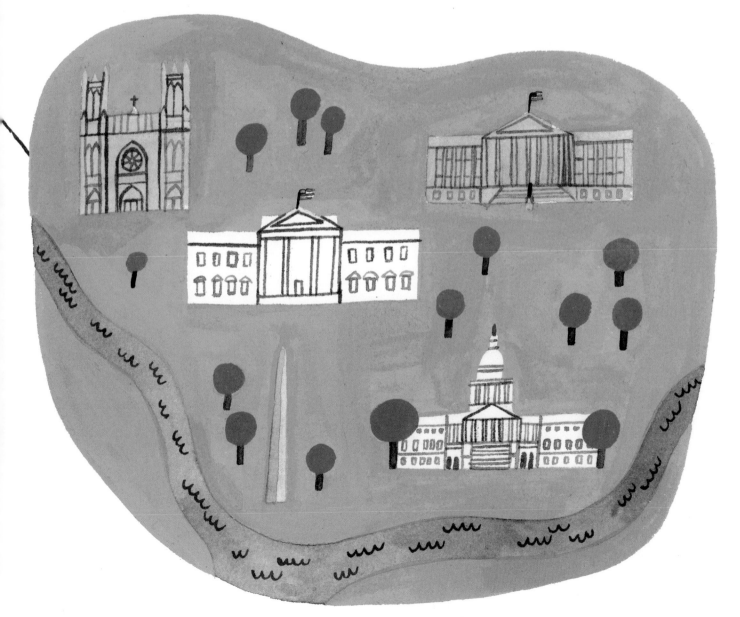

WASHINGTON, D.C.

As much as Elizebeth enjoyed the challenges
of her job, she never forgot her love of literature.
She wanted to write books and raise a family.
With the war over, Elizebeth decided it was time
to take a break from working full time. She and
William moved out of the city.

The first book Elizebeth wrote was about codes and ciphers. She also wrote and illustrated a children's book about the history of the alphabet. While she wrote, the family pets, Crypto the dog and Pinklepurr the cat, kept her company.

But every time she found herself deep in creative thought, the doorbell rang. Again and again, another government agency needed her decoding skills.

"I am summoned by telegram to a city two or three thousand miles away, to read several thousand messages to be used in a court case the following Monday... I pack my bag and hug my children a good-by... and board a train."

GREEN MANSION

This time it was the Coast Guard at her door. The Coasties were frustrated. Prohibition laws made it illegal to sell alcohol in the United States, but smugglers didn't care. There was too much money to be made. They carried bootleg liquor on ships and hid from the authorities by coding their messages to each other.

The Coast Guard couldn't crack the codes. The so-called rumrunners were winning. Elizebeth's decoding ability was the Coast Guard's only hope to catch them. So, in 1925, she went back to work as a full-time cryptanalyst.

In her first three months of work, Elizebeth decoded *two years* of backlogged messages—using nothing but pencil and paper. She was the first person in the United States to use the new science of cryptology to catch smugglers.

"[Some of the codes were] of a complexity never attempted by any government for its most secret communications."

TOP SECRET

Elizebeth often testified at criminal trials. During the famous Consolidated Exporters case, an attorney claimed Elizebeth's decodes were her opinion and not science. To prove them wrong, Elizebeth asked for a blackboard.

On it, she wrote OLD COLONEL, a brand of liquor, and ALCOHOL, three words she had decoded from a secret message. Below, she printed the matching coded letters. The same letter in the secret message always decoded to an *O* in the plaintext. This was also true for the *L*s.

The lawyers couldn't deny the evidence before their eyes.

"Cryptanalysis has its dull moments, and even despairing ones. On the other hand, when I have struggled for long, weary hours... on a problem that has appeared utterly hopeless and then suddenly burst through to light and a successful solution, then the work has its thrills."

Elizebeth's evidence helped convict twenty-five smugglers, all of whom received the maximum sentence. After this case, everyone knew that cryptology, or code breaking, was definitely a science, not fantasy. And that Elizebeth was an expert in the field.

Elizebeth and her assistant struggled to keep up with the piles of work. It was clear the Coast Guard needed a better system, not to mention more code breakers, so Elizebeth created the Coast Guard's first code-breaking unit. She staffed it with people she personally trained.

As a break from long hours of tedious work, Elizebeth spent weekends digging in the flower garden with her children, John Ramsay and Barbara. Evenings, she might attend the theater or play piano in a musical quartet, but cryptography was never far from her mind.

"When decoding, the skeletons of words leap out, and make you jump."

In 1938, she and William held an unusual dinner party. They hosted each course at a different restaurant. Instead of telling their colleagues the names of the restaurants, they gave clues in code. If their guests wanted to eat, they had to crack the code!

At work, Elizebeth and her team continued to break code after code—often in foreign languages.

The United States had entered World War II, and the Office of Strategic Services (OSS) had a huge problem. They had gathered secret communications from around the world, but they were all in code. In order to keep our nation safe, they needed to know what those messages said.

"Many times I've been asked as to how my direction, that is, the direction and superior status of a woman as instructor, teacher, mentor... how these men accepted my authority."

Since the OSS didn't have a code-breaking unit in 1942, it was up to Elizebeth to create one. She couldn't find enough people trained in cryptology, so she hired mathematicians, physicists, and chemists. She knew scientists could think analytically, a skill needed for code breaking. Although Elizebeth was a demanding instructor, her students greatly respected her abilities and quickly learned to solve codes.

Thanks to Elizebeth, the OSS—now known as the Central Intelligence Agency (CIA)—had their first cryptography department. Elizebeth's team decoded messages from Mexico and South America that contained secret war information like the number of planes and the movement of warships. And they were in German. Once again, Elizebeth had discovered messages from Nazi spies!

The FBI director was eager to catch the spies, but Elizebeth thought they should wait until the military could learn more of the enemy's secrets. The director ignored her suggestion and ordered a raid.

Not all of the spies were captured, and the ones who escaped scurried away. Their codes had been broken, so of course they immediately changed them. This made their messages much harder to decrypt.

The FBI director grabbed all the credit for deciphering the codes and capturing the spies. Elizebeth and her team received none. She patriotically continued to crack codes for the FBI, never receiving the recognition she deserved.

"The experience of war had taught everyone that codes must be... changed very frequently."

Soon after Elizebeth helped to capture the Nazi spies, the United States Postal Service needed her skills. They had seized letters from a suspected American spy, Velvalee Dickinson. On the surface, her letters appeared to be about buying and selling cute little dolls for children.

The letters were written in readable English, or open code. The more Elizebeth studied them, the more she suspected they were really about secret warship movements. Soon she was certain that *family* referred to the enemy fleet of the Japanese warlords, and *three English dolls* were three classes of British warships.

Velvalee Dic
New York

Little boy = warship
Three English dolls = three
British warship
Fisherman with net =
minesweeper
Old woman with wood
warship with supe

Elizebeth had broken the code and provided proof that Dickinson was a spy. The "Doll Lady" pled guilty to working for the Japanese. Because of Elizebeth's hard work, the war's "Number One Woman Spy" was sentenced to ten years in prison.

"It is obvious that even a casual examination of these letters indicates their suspicious nature."

"All the countries of the world were trying to develop something that nobody else could read and make sense out of."

Then came messages that used ciphers created by Enigma, the advanced German code-making machine. With its rotating wheels, Enigma could create billions of different cipher alphabets. Every letter in the message was coded using a different alphabet. Cryptanalysts around the world raced to solve the tough Enigma codes.

Just when it seemed Elizebeth and her team would never beat Enigma, they got a lucky break. A lazy Enigma operator didn't bother changing the start position of the wheels for each new message. The machine produced the same alphabets over and over again. This was the opportunity Elizebeth's group needed.

"This is the latest
in a series of messages
dealing with the attempt
of the German
espionage ring to
form an anti-U.S. bloc."

It wasn't easy, and took months of work, but Elizebeth's team finally broke the supposedly unbreakable Enigma codes. Because of wartime secrecy, they didn't know that others (such as a British team led by now-famous code breaker Alan Turing) had also broken the codes.

Alan Turing

It was a bad time for the Nazis. How had Americans found out so many of their military secrets? Everyone knew the Enigma code was unbeatable. It was as if someone were eavesdropping on secret Nazi conversations. And in a way, Elizebeth and her team were doing just that.

German secret messages were no longer secret.

"There were adventures as the minds and attempting to spy United

Decoded transmissions gave the military advance warning of the Nazis' planned attacks and bombing raids. Historians are certain that by breaking the Enigma codes, Elizebeth and other code breakers in Allied countries around the world saved thousands of lives and shortened the war by many years.

exciting, round-the-clock we counter-spied into activities of the agents into those of the States."

Elizebeth knew how important it was to keep her work hush-hush. After all, lives depended on the enemy not knowing what she was doing. Because of this, the government classified all her work Top Secret Ultra and placed it under lock and key in the National Archives. They threatened to put Elizebeth in jail if she spoke about her accomplishments, even to her husband, her children, or her six grandchildren. The government made her swear she would never tell anyone—and she never did.

The last of Elizebeth's secrets were finally declassified in 2015, thirty-five years after her death.

"[My work involved] detective stories of high interest in many cases,

Elizebeth was a true heroine of both World War I and World War II. She is now considered one of the most gifted and influential code breakers of all time. Yet no one knew how many codes she broke, how many Nazis she stopped, how many American lives she saved . . . until now.

CODES AND CIPHERS

Cryptology is the scientific study of codes and ciphers. **Cryptographers** or **code makers** create **cryptograms**, strings of text that have been made unreadable by the use of either a code or a cipher. **Cryptanalysts** or **code breakers** decrypt cryptograms into **plaintext**, a message that can be read and understood by anyone, either before it is encoded or after decoding.

A **code** creates a relationship between two groups of symbols or letters. Codes are all around us. For example, the texting abbreviation LOL is code for the phrase "laugh out loud." Elizebeth's nickname, Elsbeth, is code for her real name. A logo, like the symbol on a pair of sneakers, is code for a specific company. Some codes are public, like the ones above, and some are secret. For the secret ones, you need a **codebook**. This is a dictionary that gives the meaning of all codes used by a group of people.

An **open code** uses readable words to hide the fact the message contains secret content.

In a **cipher**, each character in a message is replaced by another character. The simplest one is a **mono-alphabetic substitution**, where each letter or number is always replaced by the same character, no matter where it appears in the message.

An example of this is the **Caesar cipher**, used throughout this book. In this case, each letter in the plaintext is created by shifting the letters in the cryptogram a specific number of positions to the left or right. For example, if the secret rule, or **key**, is to shift each letter one position to the right on the alphabet, you can send and receive messages like the following:

If your plaintext message is: **S E C R E T**

and you shift the letters one position to the right,

it creates the unreadable cryptogram: **T F D S F U**

If the receiver shifts the letters back one position left,

it creates the readable plaintext: **S E C R E T**

In a **running key cipher**, the number of positions to shift changes with each letter in the message. The sender needs to get these numbers to the receiver for each secret message. One way to do this is with a **book cipher**, where both parties have a copy of the same book. All the sender needs to do is to tell the receiver on what page and word to start.

This creates a **poly-alphabetic substitution**, which is harder to crack. Now, the same letter or number in the message does not always code to the same character. If an *E* codes to an *F* in one place in the message, elsewhere it might code to an *X* or a *Q* or some other letter.

Machines, like **Enigma**, used alphabets on rotating wheels to create poly-alphabetic substitutions. By changing the starting position of the wheels, Enigma could produce many billions of codes. But even the toughest coded messages in the world can be deciphered by knowing the correct keys.

YV IXROFB TXIIJXOH FIIRPQOXQBA YV YOLL YV YOLL

CRACK THE CODE!

OBXAFKD XKA TOFQFKD PBZOBQ JBPPXDBP FP
BXPV LKZB VLR EXSB ZOXZHBA QEB ZLAB.

Do you want to be a code breaker like Elizebeth? Here's your chance. Above is a secret message coded using a Caesar cipher. Follow these steps and crack the code:

1. Write the letters of the alphabet, A to Z, at the top of a blank sheet of paper.

2. Carefully copy the letters of the secret message written above onto the paper. Make sure you leave room beneath the letters to write.

3. Look through the secret message and figure out which letter occurs the most times. Circle that letter wherever it appears in the message. Since the most common letter in the English language is *E*, that letter probably decodes to an *E*.

4. We have to start somewhere, so let's guess that it does code to an *E*. Write *E* below each circled letter in the secret message.

5. Next, figure out the number of letters the cipher shifts between the coded message and the plaintext. To do this, find your circled letter on the alphabet at the top of the page. Count the number of letters you have to go to the right to get to the letter *E*.

6. For each letter in the secret message, count the same number of letters to the right on the alphabet to find the decoded letter. Write the new letter below the coded one in the secret message.

7. If your counting takes you past *Z*, go back to *A* and keep counting.

8. Did you crack the code? Congratulations! Now try writing your own secret message using a Caesar cipher.

CRYPTOGRAPHY TODAY

Cryptography has come a long way since Elizebeth Friedman's time. Coded messages are now part of our everyday life. If they weren't coded, anyone could snoop into private emails and texts or steal online gaming and shopping information.

These days, software encrypts and decrypts (codes and decodes) much of the information sent over the Internet. Cryptographic programs use keys, stored in a computer file, that contain hundreds of bits (0s and 1s). Keys are like your passwords, but *much* longer.

Here's an example of how these keys work. Let's say Alice wants to send a secret message to her friend Bob, but she's worried Eve might read it. (Alice and Bob are names commonly used by cryptographers. Eve, or the eavesdropper, is the person who wants to listen in.)

There are two types of keys—secret or public. With secret keys, Alice's software encrypts the message using the same key that Bob's does to decrypt it. But there's a big problem. How can Alice and Bob send each other that key without Eve stealing it?

That's why modern cryptographic software uses public keys—ones that anyone can know. Computer software creates a public key for people and organizations by multiplying two extremely large numbers together. That software keeps track of both the public key and the private numbers used to create it. Any messages sent are now safe, because it's almost impossible to figure out the original numbers by knowing only the public key.

When Alice wants to send her note to Bob using a public key, she enters it into the messaging or email software. Her software reaches out to Bob's in what is called a "handshake," to find out Bob's public key. It then uses this key to encrypt Alice's message. Even if Eve somehow gets ahold of it, all she'll see is gibberish.

Since Bob's software knows his two original numbers, it can decrypt the gibberish back into plain text. Eve has no way of finding out these secret numbers. Alice's message is safe from prying eyes.

But the best encryption software in the world won't keep your messages and online activities safe if you're not careful. You alone are responsible for your passwords. It's important to keep your passwords private. Don't use your dog's name or your birthdate or any piece of information that could be found online!

It's very important to use different passwords for different websites. If hackers break into an online site, they might steal your password. That's pretty bad, and you'd better change your password again right away. But if you've used that same password somewhere else—watch out! The hacker can log in everywhere you can.

It's also important to create long passwords that contain numbers, letters, and symbols. This makes it harder for people to guess them. For example, if you have a password that's only four numbers long, it won't take a hacker long to crack it. Within just a few minutes that person can not only see, but also mess with, all your personal information. Yikes!

Cryptography is always evolving. Software engineers add more and more features to programs to make it tougher to hack the encryptions. Some websites now offer two-factor authentication. This is like having two separate keys. The first key is your private password. The second key is created by the website and sent to you, usually in an email or text. This way, even if hackers steal your password, they can't log in and pretend to be you, because they don't have the second key.

TIMELINE

August 26, 1892
Elizebeth Smith is born in Huntington, Indiana

1914
World War I starts

Spring 1915
Graduates Hillsdale College in Michigan

1916–1920
Works for George Fabyan at Riverbank Laboratories in Geneva, Illinois

April 6, 1917
United States enters World War I

May 1917
Marries William F. Friedman

1917–1918
Decodes secret messages for the U.S. Army

1918
World War I ends

1920
Prohibition starts

1921–1922
Works for the Army Signal Corps

1922–1927
Consults part time as a cryptanalyst

October 14, 1923
Daughter Barbara is born

July 28, 1926
Son John Ramsay is born

1927–1946
Works as a cryptanalyst for the Coast Guard and the Treasury Department

1930
Receives a master's degree in archeology

1931
Founds an elite code-breaking unit for the Coast Guard

1933
Helps break up the Consolidated Exporters liquor smuggling ring

1933
Prohibition ends

1938
Receives an honorary doctorate from Hillsdale College

1939
World War II starts

1940–1942
Helps break up Nazi spy rings in New York, Mexico, and South America

December 7, 1941
United States enters World War II

December 1942
Enigma code is cracked

1942
Creates the first cryptography unit in the OSS, now the CIA

1944
Helps break up the Doll Lady's spy ring

1945
World War II ends

1945
Elizebeth's files are classified TOP SECRET ULTRA and locked in the National Archives in Washington, D.C.

October 31, 1980
Elizebeth Smith Friedman dies at age 88 in Plainfield, New Jersey

1999
Inducted into the National Security Agency (NSA) Cryptologic Hall of Honor

2002
NSA OPS1 building dedicated as the William and Elizebeth Friedman Building

2014
Justice Department auditorium dedicated to Elizebeth as a pioneer of intelligence-led policing

October 2015
The last of Elizebeth's secret files are declassified and finally made public

April 2019
U.S. Senate passes a resolution honoring the "life and legacy of Elizebeth Smith Friedman, Cryptanalyst"